The Forbidden Grief

Peter Barnes

Tulip Publishing

The Forbidden Grief

This Edition: 2019

For information contact:

Tulip Publishing, PO Box 3150, Lansvale, NSW, Australia 2166

www.tulippublishing.com.au

Book and Cover design by Tulip Publishing

PAPERBACK ISBN: 978-0-6485399-3-3

Ptinted in the United States

The Forbidden Grief

You have had an abortion. You believed that in the circumstances it was the best thing. They told you that it was just a bunch of cells in your body. They never used the word 'baby' - it was the 'product of conception', a 'foetus', or even just 'body tissue' or a 'blob'. You were not counselled; you were shovelled along in a predetermined direction. It had more to do with sales techniques than with counselling.

You wanted to believe that an abortion would be a safe and legal minor operation—a 'termination', they said—and that you would soon recover and be back to normal. You listened to the experts who told you that abortion is a relatively benign procedure, both medically and psychologically. They said—if they mentioned the possibility at all—that the number of women who suffer significant emotional distress after abortion is almost infinitesimal. Post-abortion syndrome was even labelled a 'myth', a relic of the over-sensitive Puritan conscience.

It was not too hard for you to convince yourself that abortion was the best thing in the circumstances. Indeed, it would almost be the noble thing as it would not be fair to bring a child into this troubled world, especially not at this particular time. But somehow something somewhere has gone wrong. It has not worked out for you in the way that you thought it would. Instead of relief, you feel a dull ache, regrets, and at times a terrible agony. The aftershocks have been far greater than you were led to believe.

Sin Hurts Us Deeply

The Bible tells of King David's adultery with Bathsheba, who became pregnant. In an attempt to cover up his sin, David had Bathsheba's husband, Uriah, moved to the front line of battle, where he was soon killed. For a while, David thought that he was off the hook. His sins of adultery, murder and deception had been concealed (2 Sam. 11–12).

Yet he himself knew that something had happened within his own soul. He felt unclean and dirty. And this had physical effects on him—he was in pain, he had no strength, he felt drained, and he could not sleep. Life was not the same for David. He records: 'When I kept silent, my bones wasted away through my groaning all day long. For day and night Your hand was heavy upon me; my strength was sapped as in the heat of summer' (Ps. 32:3–4). Sin had made David dysfunctional. He tried desperately to smother his fears, stifle his conscience, and delude his mind.

No doubt some of David's courtiers thought that he had caught a virus. Perhaps others said: 'Time heals all wounds. You will soon get over the episode with Bathsheba and the death of Uriah.' Maybe the royal psychologist told him to try to get rid of his feelings of guilt by taking up a hobby. But we have feelings of guilt because we are objectively guilty before God. To take away our feelings of guilt, we need the guilt itself to be taken away. For twelve months or so, David was haunted by what he had done. The sweet singer of Israel, the man after God's own heart, had become sullen and heavy, with no heart for life.

And so it is with abortion. All kinds of unforeseen consequences come from having an abortion. You tried not to think about it, to put it behind you, and get on with life, but it has been hard, surprisingly hard. You may have felt depressed, useless and isolated. Life has been a burden, with bouts of uncontrolled crying, and even panic attacks. Sleep brings little relief; there are dreams of babies, and, what is worse, nightmares. It is difficult to look at a young mother with her child.

You think of what you might have had, and should have had. You remember the date on which your baby would have been born. You fantasise about babies. One woman put it like this: 'Sometimes I open my arms and embrace the air'. Or: 'In my mind, I have a son I cannot touch and cannot feed and who follows me about like a ghost.'

Perhaps you now hate your husband or your partner. He should have protected you, but instead he pressured you into thinking you had to go through with the termination. Or maybe he just abdicated and left you alone to make the fateful decision. Maybe your relationship has even broken up. Something like 80% of relationships do not survive an abortion. The baby is not the only victim. One woman who had an abortion became so embittered that she laughed when she heard that her abortionist's daughter had been murdered. Abortion damages our integrity as human beings. One woman wrote: 'I have terminated myself.'

This is the grief you were not supposed to feel. They told you that abortion was safer, both psychologically and medically, than childbirth. Yet now this is the loneliest grief of all. There are no photos, no little reminders of past joys, no shared memories, and no grave to visit. To the outsider there is nothing, but to you the reality is very different. Now even your happiest moments are shadowed by a secret sadness. People grieve greatly —and sometimes feel guilty—even after a miscarriage, but it is so much worse after an abortion. With an abortion, grief is mixed with real objective guilt.

You may have felt so cheap and worthless that you took to a promiscuous lifestyle. Perhaps drugs or alcohol have become too much a part of your life. Your whole personality has changed, but you have tried to keep up some kind of facade. Even the sexual act—the place where all life begins—has become a painful reminder of the life you did not bring to fruition. Perhaps you have become so desperate that you have thought of suicide. Sometimes the reaction can be delayed, but it can be severe and prolonged. Never in all your life have you felt so empty and desolate.

It is strange—you may not have thought of yourself as a very religious person, yet you feel overcome by guilt and pain. At the bar of God, the giver of life, you stand condemned. Activities dull the pain for a time, but when you are alone, the memories haunt you. Grief often comes in waves. You may feel that you can never be forgiven. People who are close to you tell you to forget it, but those are mocking words. There may be smiles and platitudes from those who know your secret, but these bring no real comfort. You would love another chance; you would do anything to wipe the slate clean and do it right this time.

The Joy of Forgiveness

You may have tried all sorts of remedies to make up for what you have done or at least to cope with the horrible feeling inside you. Perhaps you have tried to fall pregnant again, as soon as possible. Or maybe you have adopted a sponsorship child, who has become a kind of replacement or atonement child. Sometimes women adopt a baby's gravesite and visit it, especially on the birthday of the aborted baby. It is common—and helpful, no doubt—to name the aborted child. A kind of funeral service—or farewell ceremony—can be held. People even try to find consolation by praying for, or even to, the dead child. These days many people try to pretend that we are able to forgive ourselves.

The breakthrough for David came in his confession of his sin to God: 'I acknowledged my sin to You, and I did not cover my iniquity; I said, "I will confess my transgressions to the Lord," and you forgave the iniquity of my sin.' (Ps. 32:5). This is the key to it all. This is what all of Scripture teaches: 'If we confess our sins, He [God] is faithful and just to forgive us our sins and to cleanse us from all unrighteousness' (1 John 1:9). The way up is first to go down.

As Augustine of Hippo put it: 'What we need is true confession, not false defence.' That is what David realised: 'I brought my sin to God, I stopped pretending and playing games, I brought it openly to God in confession, and He forgave me. I was not put on probation; I was freely forgiven.' When Christ died on the cross, He satisfied the justice of God and paid the full penalty for sin. He paid the debt which you owe to God. This having been done, so He freely offers mercy to all who come to Him in repentance and faith (Rom. 3:21–26).

When David turned to God again, he knew what it was to be cleared in the court of heaven. He was indeed guilty, but now he was acquitted, freed and clean. He found forgiveness the only way that it can be found—through repentance and faith in the One who gave His life for the wrong things we have done.

The hymn-writer, Fanny Crosby, sang of this grace:

The vilest offender who truly believes,

That moment from Jesus a pardon receives.

David knew the misery of sin, and also the joy of forgiveness. You know the misery, but you can also know the joy. Your terrible grief may in fact open the door to unimaginable joy. It may be a sign that God is indeed calling you to Himself. As Thomas Watson put it: 'We are never more precious in God's eyes than when we are lepers in our own.'

In thc New Testament we read the account of a woman who was a sinner—almost certainly a prostitute—who washed Jesus' feet with her tears and dried them with her hair. Jesus declared that she was forgiven her many, many sins. Her response was to be very, very grateful (Luke 7:36–53).

A Life Restored

In confessing his sin to God, David found that his life was put back together. The holy God had forgiven the unholy David. As we saw earlier, those who are forgiven much love much (Luke 7:47). They have every reason to lift their voices in praise of God's grace.

Instead of hiding in shame from God, David is now secure in His love and protection, no matter what troubles might come his way. When he refused to acknowledge his sin before God, he moped around in abject misery; now he can shout for joy. He has a message for others which has been ratified by his own experience: 'Therefore let everyone who is godly offer prayer to you at a time when you may be found; surely in the rush of great waters, they shall not reach him. You are a hiding place for me; you preserve me from trouble; you surround me with shouts of deliverance.' (Ps. 32:6–7).

How David has changed! He had been hiding from God, but now God is his hiding place. Now he prays, now he is secure in God's love and protection, now he is protected no matter what flood of calamities come his way, now he is full of praise—he cannot help but sing out loud to the God who has redeemed him. Freed from sin, David now fears nothing.

David learnt his lesson: 'Many are the sorrows of the wicked, but steadfast love surrounds the one who trusts in the Lord. Be glad in the Lord, and rejoice, O righteous, and shout for joy, all you upright in heart!' (Ps. 32:10–11)! The world thinks that God is in the business of promoting misery and that sin is somehow related to happiness. The truth, which you yourself have already experienced in part, is that sin breeds misery but forgiveness brings joy and delight.

David wrote this Psalm under the inspiration of God so that the likes of you and me would know how to deal with our sins. You cannot pretend that abortion is a non-event, like the clipping of your toenails. David had blood on his hands, but he found that God was more gracious than he could ever have believed. You have shed innocent blood in sin; Christ shed His innocent blood to atone for sin.

The Lord is rich and merciful;
The Lord is very kind;
O come to Him, come now to Him,
With a believing mind.
His comforts, they shall strengthen thee,
Like flowing waters cool;
And He shall for thy spirit be
A fountain ever full.

That was David's experience. God calls you to make it yours too.

As he was dying in the year AD 430, Augustine of Hippo read from copies of some of the Psalms which he had placed on his bedroom walls. One of the Psalms which he read was this one—Psalm 32. Augustine wept as he thought of his own sins and the undeserved mercy of God. He knew the truth of the gospel, expressed in his own words: 'Let a man grieve for his sin and rejoice for his grief.'

You may, however, have one last question: 'God offers me forgiveness and cleansing, but what about the child I aborted?' When David committed adultery with Bathsheba, she fell pregnant. In the aftermath of Uriah's death, the prophet

Nathan confronted David about his sin. David was shattered: 'I have sinned against the Lord' (2 Sam. 12:13). Nathan went on to declare God's forgiveness of David, and that the king would not die, but he also said that the young child would die. For seven days, David was absorbed in sorrow—he wept, fasted and prayed that the life of the child would be spared.

All to no avail, as the child died. It was then, however, that David said: 'I shall go to him, but he will not return to me' (2 Sam. 12:23). Death is a one-way street. Yes, the child was dead. But one day David too would die and be reunited with his child in glory. Christ died to pay the death penalty for sinners, but He also rose from the dead, never to die again. Sin and death have been overcome for all who repent of their sins and cast themselves upon the mercy of Christ. Then, as the Scripture says, 'death is swallowed up in victory' (1 Cor. 15:54). Your forbidden grief can become endless victory, but only in Christ.

Ashlie's Story

The test was positive. There I was, fifteen and pregnant. After we left a doctor, my mother suddenly remembered I'd had a rubella vaccination recently. The gynaecologist said the baby would be deformed. An abortion was necessary.

So, shortly afterwards, there I was in hospital not pregnant any more. My tears just wouldn't stop.

This episode unfortunately taught me a lesson. If you don't want a baby, you 'get rid of it'.

Years later, in my twenties, I was pregnant again. I was so profligate I don't even remember the father. It was a simple matter to go to a doctor I knew personally and ask him to end it. He did as I asked. Still I hadn't learned the real lesson.

I was far from being a Christian in those days, I didn't even know any Christians. The thought of 'Thou Shalt Not Kill' didn't enter my head. After all, babies aren't people until they're born, so I thought.

In my thirties, I was living with a long-term partner and we didn't want any children. I was too careless about taking the pill and fell pregnant again. Abortions still weren't that easy to to get but I knew if I pressed my doctor, he would recommend a clinic where I could go. After all, I was a drug addict, and nobody wants a baby born to one of those, do they? He complied.

These last two abortions didn't turn a hair on my head. My problems were solved so easily.

In my early forties, my girlfriend came to me when she fell pregnant to a married man. She didn't want it either, so I took her to the same doctor with the same result.

It was all too easy.

In my mid-forties, it all started to catch up with me. My lifestyle came home to roost. My drug taking and men drove me away for a few weeks to a safe haven. While there, the Holy Spirit began working in me. I was psychotic and didn't know it. I was also physically ill. I started going to church.

When I came back to Sydney my mess of a life crowded in. In hospital I started to read the Bible. I began to realise what I had done taking all those lives.

I cried to God for days, begging him to forgive me for what I had done. Now I have given my life to Jesus, I believe I have been forgiven.

Nothing, however, will ever remove the regret I feel. I can only hope that one day, I will meet the souls of those little mites in heaven.

Psalm 32

Blessed is the one whose transgression
is forgiven, whose sin is covered.

Blessed is the man against whom
the Lord counts no iniquity, and in
whose spirit there is no deceit.

For when I kept silent, my bones wasted
away through my groaning all day long.

For day and night your hand was
heavy upon me; my strength was
dried up as by the heat of summer.

I acknowledged my sin to you, and
I did not cover my iniquity;

I said, "I will confess my
transgressions to the Lord," and you
forgave the iniquity of my sin.

Therefore let everyone who is
godly offer prayer to you at a time
when you may be found;

surely in the rush of great waters,
they shall not reach him.

You are a hiding place for me; you
preserve me from trouble; you surround
me with shouts of deliverance.

I will instruct you and teach you in
the way you should go; I will counsel
you with my eye upon you.

Be not like a horse or a mule, without
understanding, which must be curbed with
bit and bridle, or it will not stay near you.

Many are the sorrows of the wicked,
but steadfast love surrounds the
one who trusts in the Lord.

Be glad in the Lord, and rejoice,
O righteous, and shout for joy,
all you upright in heart!

Resources

Pregnancy Support

Australia:

New South Wales

Diamond Women's Support (Sydney)

1300 851 592

https://diamondwomensupport.com

Hope House (Sydney)

0433 930 220

http://hopehouse.com.au

Lily Rose Pregnancy Support (Coff's Harbour)

0423 227 917

https://lilyrose.org.au

Queensland

Eva's Place (Toowoomba)

07 4642 1910

http://evasplace.org.au

South Australia

Birthline Pregnancy Support (Adelaide)

1300 655 156

https://birthline.org.au

Genesis Pregnancy Services (Adelaide)

08 8352 4044

http://genesispregnancysupport.org.au

Pregnancy Help SA (Adelaide)

0403 760 200

http://pregnancyhelpsa.com.au

Victoria

Open Doors Counselling (Melbourne)

1800 647 995

http://opendoors.com.au

Western Australia

Pregnancy Matters

Albany: 08 9842 1572 | Rockingham: 08 9518 2698

http://pregnancymatters.org.au

Canada:

Birthright (National)

1800 550 4900

https://birthright.org

Anchor of Hope Pregnancy and Family Care Centre (Ontario)

613-473-0606

http://anchorofhope.ca

Pregnancy Help Centre of Durham (Ontario)

905-720-3252 / 905-619-9878

http://pregnancyhelp.ca

New Zealand:

Gianna's Choice (Auckland / Wellington)

0800 367 5433

http://pregnancyoptions.org.nz

United Kingdom:

Life (National)

0808 802 5433

http://lifecharity.org.uk

United States:

OptionLine (National)

313131

https://optionline.org

Post-Abortion Support

Australia:

New South Wales

Diamond Women's Support (Sydney)

1300 851 592

https://diamondwomensupport.com

Queensland

Eva's Place (Toowoomba)

07 4642 1910

http://evasplace.org.au

South Australia

Genesis Pregnancy Services (Adelaide)

08 8352 4044

http://genesispregnancysupport.org.au

Canada:

Post Abortion Community Services (British Columbia)

604-525-0999

http://pacscanada.org

Pregnancy Help Centre of Durham (Ontario)

905-720-3252 / 905-619-9878

http://pregnancyhelp.ca

United Kingdom:

Life (National)

0808 802 5433

http://lifecharity.org.uk

United States:

Abortion Recovery InterNational (National)

866-721-7781

http://abortionrecovery.org

Healing Hearts Ministries (National)

505-355-6922

https://healinghearts.org

SaveOne (National)

615-347-8800

https://saveone.org

Surrending The Secret (National)

https://surrenderingthesecret.com

Organisations

Australia:

Evangelicals For Life

http://evangelicalsforlife.com

LifeChoices

https://lifechoice.org.au

United Kingdom

Society for the Protection of Unborn Children

https://spuc.org.uk

United States

Abort73

https://abort73.com

Human Coalition

https://www.humancoalition.org